Grateful & Blessed Stress THANKSGIVING stress relief coloring pages for adults

An Inspirational Large-Print Thanksgiving Coloring Book for Adults and Seniors Simple Designs • Mindful Moments • Autumn Comforts

Margaret Lane

Chapter 1

⭐ What Readers Are Saying

"Soothing and sweet — exactly what I needed." *The simple designs are easy on my eyes and hands, and the quotes were genuinely calming. I've already gifted one to my mom!*

— Marjorie T., 67, retired teacher

"My mother with dementia loves it." *The large print and simple pages are perfect. She colors while I read the quotes aloud — it's become a peaceful ritual for us both.*

— Laura M., caregiver & daughter

"A beautiful reminder to slow down." *The mix of cozy scenes, inspirational quotes, and gratitude reflections made this feel like self-care on every page.*

— Nina R., 44, social worker

Margaret Lane

"Simple enough for seniors, thoughtful enough for everyone." *I often struggle with coloring books — but this one was perfect. Large print, bold lines, and themes of peace and thankfulness.*

— Henry L., 72, retired veteran

"Perfect Thanksgiving gift." *My aunt said it felt like a warm hug and brought back happy memories. A thoughtful and meaningful gift.*

— Tasha B., 36, family caregiver

Welcome to Grateful & Blessed

A Large-Print Thanksgiving Coloring Book for Adults

Welcome — we're so happy you're here.

This book was thoughtfully designed for anyone who enjoys the peace of coloring but prefers **large, easy-to-see designs**. Whether you're a senior, someone with visual challenges, or simply looking for a relaxing and uplifting activity, this book is made with you in mind.

Inside, you'll find calming autumn scenes, heartfelt gratitude quotes, and joyful Thanksgiving imagery — all with **bold lines, simple shapes**, and **plenty of space to color comfortably**. There's no need to stay inside the lines or rush. Just enjoy the process.

Some pages are just for coloring, while others invite you to reflect or write a few thoughts if you'd like. But there are no rules here — use this book in whatever way feels most enjoyable and peaceful to you.

Welcome to Grateful & Blessed

Take a moment to pause, reflect, and fill these pages with your colors of gratitude.

Wishing you comfort, creativity, and many moments of joy as you color.

With appreciation,

The Grateful & Blessed Team

How to Use This Book

This coloring book is designed to be **simple, relaxing, and easy to enjoy** — no matter your experience level or eyesight.

Here are a few friendly tips to help you get the most out of it:

Choose What Speaks to You

Flip through the pages and pick one that feels right for the moment — a comforting quote, a peaceful scene, or a space to write what you're thankful for.

Use What You Like

Colored pencils, markers, crayons — anything works! Just make sure to place a blank sheet of paper behind the page if your colors might bleed through.

How to Use This Book

Enjoy the Large Print & Bold Lines

All designs are created with **clear, bold outlines and large-print text**, perfect for easier visibility and stress-free coloring.

Go at Your Own Pace

There's no rush. This book is here to help you slow down, breathe deeply, and enjoy each moment of creativity.

Reflect, Color, or Just Relax

Some pages include prompts to help you reflect on what brings you joy and gratitude. Feel free to write — or simply color and enjoy the calming imagery.

This is your time to relax, reflect, and feel good. Do what brings you peace.

A Note of Thanks to You

Thank you for spending time with *Grateful & Blessed*. We hope these pages brought you a sense of calm, comfort, and connection — and maybe even a smile or two along the way. Whether you colored one page or many, took time to reflect, or simply enjoyed the quiet moments, we're truly grateful you chose to share this journey with us. **"Joy is not in things; it is in us." — Richard Wagner** . As you move forward, may you carry with you the simple joy of creating, the peace of reflection, and the power of gratitude. The beauty you bring to the world — with your colors, your thoughts, your presence — is something to be celebrated every day. Stay kind to yourself, stay curious, and keep seeking joy in the little things.

With heartfelt thanks,

The Grateful & Blessed Team

ABUNDANCE BEGINS WITH GRATITUDE

"The Little Things We Often Miss"

Sometimes, we look for big moments to be thankful for — holidays, milestones, grand gestures. But more often, gratitude grows in the small and quiet things: the warmth of a blanket, the smell of something baking, the golden light of late afternoon. These little things are always with us, waiting to be noticed. When we pause and pay attention, we often find we have more than we thought — and more peace than we expected.

Grateful.
Thankful.
Blessed.

Made with love, shared with thanks.

"Permission to Pause"

The world can be fast and loud. But this book isn't. This is your space to slow down. To breathe a little deeper. To let your mind wander gently — without judgment or hurry. Whether you color one leaf or a whole page, you've taken time for yourself, and that matters. You don't have to be productive every second. Sometimes, rest is the most important thing you can do.

TAKE TIME TO REST, REFLECT, AND BE GRATEFUL.

_____

_____

_____

"The Beauty of Letting Go"

As the leaves turn and fall, nature reminds us that change can be beautiful. Autumn doesn't resist the wind — it dances with it. There is wisdom in this season. It teaches us to let go, to gather what matters, and to make room for rest and reflection. In this quiet turning of the year, we find space for gratitude — not because everything is perfect, but because there is still so much good around us.

PEOPLE I AM GRATEFUL FOR...

THANKFUL TREE

_____
_____
_____

"A Cup of Comfort"

Maybe it's a soft sweater you always reach for. Maybe it's the sound of laughter in another room, or a recipe that tastes like childhood. Comfort doesn't have to be big. It lives in small moments that feel familiar and safe. Coloring can be one of those moments. Like a warm mug between your hands, it brings a sense of quiet presence. These are the kinds of moments that fill us up — gently, quietly, fully.

"Thankful Anyway"

Some days are easier than others. Some years are harder than we ever expected. But even on the tough days, we can often find one small thing to hold onto — a kind word, a memory, a ray of light through the window. Gratitude doesn't mean pretending everything is perfect. It means choosing to notice the good, even if it's just a little at a time. And that choice, over and over again, brings us strength.

"Creating Calm"

There's something special about coloring. It quiets the mind and softens the edges of the day. The colors you choose don't have to be realistic or perfect — they only need to feel right to you. Every stroke is a way to express care, to bring beauty into the world, even if only for yourself. You're not just filling a page — you're giving yourself a moment of peace. And that is a beautiful thing.

"Grateful & Blessed — and Still Becoming"

Gratitude isn't a destination — it's a way of seeing. You don't have to feel it every second. You only have to return to it when you can. The fact that you picked up this book says something beautiful about you: that you're someone who chooses peace, creativity, and care. And no matter where you are in life, there is always more to notice, more to love, more to become. You are both grateful and growing — and that is enough.

Happy Thanksgiving

"When the Leaves Fell Slower"

Do you remember the sound of leaves crunching under your shoes when you were little? The smell of wood smoke in the air? Back then, autumn seemed to stretch out forever — full of raked leaf piles, warm mittens, and steamy windows. Even now, a whiff of cinnamon or a glimpse of golden trees can take us right back. Those memories stay tucked inside us, like favorite sweaters folded for next season. And sometimes, coloring a page brings them right back to life.

"The Table Is Big Enough"

Thanksgiving isn't just about what's on the table — it's about who's around it. Over the years, the faces may change, the dishes may shift, and the stories might get told a few more times than necessary. But one thing stays the same: there's always room for one more. One more plate, one more laugh, one more moment of connection. Whether you're seated at a bustling table or remembering those who once were, the spirit of togetherness never really leaves. It just grows quieter — and deeper.

"Gathered Blessings"

We spend much of life moving — forward, faster, onward. But the season of harvest reminds us to gather what we've grown. Not just the things we planted in soil, but the kindness we gave, the strength we found, the love we received. These are the blessings we carry with us. Gratitude isn't just a response to the good — it's a recognition of the sacred in the everyday. A warm light, a kind word, a safe place to rest. These are gifts. And they are enough.

Take time to sip, sip, slow down, and savor the season.

"Pass the Pie... Again"

Every Thanksgiving has one: the person who swears they're *too full*... and then ten minutes later, asks for "just a sliver" of pie. (Spoiler: it's never just a sliver.) But isn't that the joy of it? The second helpings, the shared desserts, the guilty giggles. It's a celebration of the moment, not the calorie count. So go ahead — pass the pie again. Life is short. And pie is worth it.

🎨 Color Test Page

Try out your favorite colors here!

Color Name / Number   **Test Box**

🎨 Try Mixing & Shading:

Use this open space to blend, layer, or try out light and dark strokes.

💡 Quick Tips:

- Place a sheet of paper behind the page when using markers.
- Try layering light colors first, then add darker tones on top.
- No pressure — this page is just for fun and experimenting!

🎨 Color Test Page

Try out your favorite colors here!

Color Name / Number	Test Box
	☐
	☐
	☐
	☐
	☐
	☐
	☐
	☐

🎨 Try Mixing & Shading:

Use this open space to blend, layer, or try out light and dark strokes.

💡 Quick Tips:

- Place a sheet of paper behind the page when using markers.
- Try layering light colors first, then add darker tones on top.
- No pressure — this page is just for fun and experimenting!

🎨 Color Test Page

Try out your favorite colors here!

Color Name / Number	Test Box
	☐
	☐
	☐
	☐
	☐
	☐
	☐
	☐

🎨 Try Mixing & Shading:

Use this open space to blend, layer, or try out light and dark strokes.

💡 Quick Tips:

- Place a sheet of paper behind the page when using markers.
- Try layering light colors first, then add darker tones on top.
- No pressure — this page is just for fun and experimenting!

www.ingramcontent.com/pod-product-compliance
Lightning Source LLC
LaVergne TN
LVHW070217080526
838202LV00067B/6838